FROM SHATTERED SPIRITS TO RESURRECTED SOULS

KIMBERLY LANELL "QUIET STORM" EDGE

Contributing writer, DeVonte' Terrell Robinson

Copyright © 2014 Kimberly Lanell Edge
Printed in USA by Greater Is He Publishing

Editor: Patrica Henderson
Interior Designer: Tony Bradford
Exterior Designer: Robert King

All rights reserved. No part of this book may be reproduced or transmitted in any form or by any means without written permission from the author.

ISBN: 978-1-938950-45-2

Greater Is He Publishing
9824 E. Washington St.
Chagrin Falls, Ohio 44023
Phone: 216.288.9315
www.GreaterIsHePublishing.com

DEDICATION

THIS BOOK IS DEDICATED TO ALL, YOUNG AND OLD, WHO HAVE FACED NUMEROUS CHALLENGES IN LIFE BUT STILL CONTINUED ON. TO ALL OF YOU WHO FEEL UNWANTED, UNAPPRECIATED AND UNLOVED: TENACITY IS ONE OF THE KEYS TO NOT ONLY SURVIVING, BUT ALSO CONQUERING.

NO MATTER HOW HARD IT GETS, NO MATTER WHAT YOU HAVE DONE, AND NO MATTER WHAT HAS BEEN DONE TO YOU, YOU CAN OVERCOME IT ALL. YOU HAVE CHOICES. MAKE THE DECISION.

WHEN YOU FEEL LIKE GIVING UP, DON'T.

YOU ARE WORTH THE FIGHT.

I BELIEVE IN YOU. PLEASE BELIEVE IN YOURSELF.

ACKNOWLEDGEMENTS

There are too many people to name. A lot of people have played a significant role in my life. They presented good and bad experiences that helped create my love of reading and writing. I have so many stories to tell. I will do so before I leave this earth through poetry, books, film, art, music, speaking engagements and any other means necessary.

My sincerest gratitude to my son, DeVonte' Terrell Robinson. You are an amazing human being and my reason for waking up each morning and continuing to move. Thank you for your understanding, love, support, challenges, laughs, and the occasional hug. We are more alike than I previously thought.

Appreciation beyond words to my mother, Euartha Lynn Edge, for everything. I thank you for being there for Boo, our Legacy. Thank you to my brother Chuckie, Grandma Sims, Grandma Edge, and Great Granny who are no longer with us. I am grateful for the memories. Thanks to my grandfathers, who left this world before I was born. I wonder if they would have been proud of me. To dad, Marvin Edge, I extend my gratitude for the sarcasm and writing influence. GP Jared, you are missed. Thank you to my other kid Tina D., my G-baby Shilo Jr., Big Shilo, my sister Nina, and my nephews Brian, Brandon, and Bryce; Ayesha, Marquel, Lil' Marquel, Big James, Lil' James, Kayla, NiNi, Lisa, Mama, Mama R. Brewer., G-Aunt, Cynthia, the Brewer and Jones family. Thank you, Christopher T. Thank you, my friend and mentor Majik Reed, Ms. Cari O., Ms. Julie B., Julia L., Ms. Michelle H., Sherry, and John.

Thank you and love to all of my family, especially my favorite aunts and uncles, and my cousins who were more like my sisters and brothers. Jackie V, Jackie E., Robin, James, Stevie, Marla, Michael, Tony, Shawn, Don, Angie, Tierra, Ta'Nylah, Shawnee, Darnasia, Jerry, Brandy, Z, Desmond, Juice, Benji, David, Kelly, Niki, and all the little cousins. If I did not name someone, don't worry; there are more books to come.

I thank my friends who have been there for me over the years and are more like family members. Thank you to the few who don't know me so well but believe in me and have been encouraging and helpful with this and many other projects.

Above all, thank you Jehovah and Jesus Christ. I am grateful for your love and understanding.

FOREWORD

Struggle. You've seen it. I've seen it. But if you are reading this, that means that you have won. If you are reading this, that means that you have lived to fight another day. So smile. Enjoy your victory. Even though the feeling of victory is a temporary one, you can still take the time and embrace it.

The author takes us through a journey of darkness and light. Of pain and pleasure. Of struggle and victory. Much of it her own.

From Shattered Spirits to Resurrected Souls is a beautifully dark scripted journey through the heart, mind, and spirit that, after reminding you where you've been, sheds the light on where you are.

My path is still filled with obstacles, but I am more prepared to maneuver. The author ensured me of that!

--Majik Reed

Note: Mr. Reed is a phenomenal father. He is friend and mentor to many; multi-award winning, Diamond selling Producer, musician, songwriter, publisher, marketing expert and entrepreneur.

Bayonne, New Jersey

CONTENTS

Section I ~ SHATTERED

Devil Within...	2
Storm..	4
They Come at Night......................................	5
Tennis Shoe...	6
The Dark Figure..	7
Victim..	8
When the Lights Went Out............................	9
The Throw-a-ways..	11
Agony..	13
Danger Lies in the Past................................	14
Lost Soul..	15
The Stone-yard..	16
Hunting Season..	17
Darkness Disguises the Sun	18
Every Day I Fight To Walk in the Eyes of the Lord	29
I Am	30

Section 2 ~ HIM, HER, THEM

Crushing...	32
Collapse...	33
Love is Not Supposed to Kill You.................	34
Transition...	35
When Will It Be?..	36
Quiet...	37
The First Time Won't be the Last.................	38
The Look, the Sound...................................	39
The Spirit...	42
Invade Her Thoughts...................................	43
Desire to Forget but not Forgive..................	45
Healing Touch..	49
Dance...	50
Helicopter...	51
Fruits of Passion..	52

Love is Not Just a Word...	53
Moves Me...	54
Forbidden..	56
Out of Reach..	57
The Other Freedom..	59
Song..	61
We Will Always Be...	62
What Feels Good	63
What You Deserve, What I Deserve.......................	68

Section 3 ~ When You Feel Like Giving Up, Don't

Resurrection – the Voice...	71
Natural, and It's Ok...	73
Never Lose Yourself..	75
Blessings..	76
Benevolence..	77

Section 4 ~ The Son – His Words

I'm Me...	79
The Forgotten...	80
Goodbye, Lebron...	81
Bright Lights...	82
Love Lost...	83
Love in Basketball...	84
Just Dance...	85
Purple Hood..	86
Stolen and Betrayed..	87
About the Author...	88

I.
SHATTERED

Devil Within

Years of looking from the inside, she saw it clearly
She imagined being outside of the hellish bubble
If only the pain could be erased.
Perhaps she would survive, nearly
The poison on her lips screamed hatred, it wasn't subtle

What she had become was what she most hated
The perfect square cubes glistened in their glass domain
Calling to her again and again. Reaching out, she had been baited.

She was tired. Weak from fighting the devil alone
No one understood the scars, the lack of strength
To control her life. Barriers destroyed a home
He was controlling her. Mental powers defiant myth

If only there wasn't so much to forgive and forget
The ringing of the phone. The devil's call.
The secret harlot, Jezebel
Whispers floating. Planning their rendezvous.
Rigid in the corner I sat
Poor woman that bore me. See it you must. Hear. I must tell

The devil's odor. Reeking of sins, suffocating, indignant
His tiny paper roll lit; ready to control
his false mental capacity
Rational intent, obscure, mentality on the brink.
Functions stagnant
Like a nymphomaniac, whorish desires, not knowing the meaning of chastity

His little children meaningless to the fire monster
Chewed and spit out to be battered by the rest of the world
Defenseless, confused, unsure of their future
unable to saunter
Always behind the wall of insecurities, waiting for the bombs to be hurled

She looked to the Heavens for power, to saw away the disease-infected limb
She was uncertain of herself, what she was to be
To dismiss all that had been and cleanse her soul of him
To kill it from the root and chop the devil's branch from her tree

3-14-1992

Storm

Rain pours heavily
Figures run for shelter
Screams over lightning
I stand in the mist of it
To be purified

2008

They Come at Night

They come at night
To feel her warmth
Watch the curves
In the darkness holding
Why do they only come
At night
Take her, take her to the sun to feel the essence of light
That which is missing in her
Cold hands sliding away from her mouth
Chastising
Looking for calm, stillness in her
Empty love, deep pits for eyes
They come at night like sad children, with open arms
To warm breasts, her strength
Looking to her sin-filled temple for shelter

1993

Tennis Shoe

The tennis shoe sat helpless
Alone
There was a red glimmer in its eyes
Terror
The tire tracks were black as tar
Screamed
The smoke still lingered from the barrel
Stench
On-lookers walked by, trying not to see
Fear
The tennis shoe's home was in the near distance
Blood
It was not quite the same, crushed and twisted
Confused
You could hear the whisper of the child
Mama
It was big brother's friend
Jealous
The child's brother was escaping this hell
Taking them to a better place
Heaven
He whispers, he can get out now, by himself
Through his soul

The Dark Figure

The dark figure stands rigid in the quiet of the night
Alone, indifferent
Emotions swirling about, there is doubt
He is strong and silent, looking for answers
Not so sure about the future. He will make a way
Wants to do so much more
Hard to trust and believe
He does not see what is before him
The one that wants the best for him
Wants the best of him
That which he does not see in himself
Impatience clouds. Uncertainty allows
Disruption, distraction, detraction
Another road is taken, another door is opened
The other one left behind to wonder
What could have been, would have been, like to have been
The dark figure moves slowly in the quiet of the night
Alone, indifferent
Masking true emotion, for what is wanted right now
He is strong and silent reaching for answers
But not touching, just a little closer and it could be

Victim

As I lay I wonder, wonder why
Where's my mom, I give out a sigh
I reach out for her but she is not there
Why do I have this feeling of despair?

Doctors around using hush-hush voices
Discussing me and all of their choices
She's sick they say, she'll never get well
Hhuumphh, I say, how can you tell

In comes a man with big brown eyes
In them all the truth lies
I cry to get my dad's attention
He talks to the doctors, about me little mention

He walks out of the room, what is this?
Leaving me here without even a kiss
I think I understand. Fear devours me
You're wrong I scream, I'll get well you'll see

Are they starving me? Is that the plan?
Who gives them the right to sit at God's right hand?
My executioners clothed in white, symbolizes purity
Come toward me, surrounds me like sharks, no dignity

One of the hypocrites speak, won't be long now
Actors claiming to be lifesavers take a bow
Suddenly I can't see, can't hear, can't move, nor cry
My last thought was a whisper, to life goodbye

When the Lights Went Out

So surprised was everyone
Bewildered
Had no idea of the darkness
Had not noticed when the light began to dim

Blinders were abundant
Family and friends
All that was seen was the smile
All that was heard was the laughter
All that was felt was the strength
All that was asked of her, was can you
And when

The brightness, the sunlight
Within, began to diminish long ago
The walls closed in
The darkness crept into her
Mind and soul
Sharp knives began to pierce at her heart
Until they began to cut away little pieces
They dropped and were shoved here and there
Stepped on and discarded
No way to find them to put them back together
The light began to narrow
No one noticed
When she became less important
To others
She retreated more into the dark corners
Each room the windows and shades began to close
The lights were turned off
She became frustrated as to how to end this
There was no concept of returning the light
To opening the doors and windows to

Letting any sunlight in
No one noticed
That she did not return
Some time had passed
The silence became deafening
One day someone noticed
It was too late
The once warm smile and light that radiated a room was
Turned into a cold expression of anguish
Midnight black permeated

Delicate fingers wrapped around the small bottles
That once held what she thought were her tiny round saviors
But once held the hands of her children
Now so cold and stiff
No one noticed
When the door closed and locked
And the lights went out

9/2012

The Throw-a-ways

The Throw-a-ways
Discarded at will
Emotions to kill
Never a warning
Never a reason
Cherished and appreciated
When others' pain is alleviated
Only for a time

Thrown in the corner
Dirty clothes on top
When needed
Digging deep to retrieve
Polished and shown off
Once again

The Throw-a-ways
Loyal, kind, dependable
Selfless, true, open, entertaining
Squeezed with love and admiration
To complete exaltation
Only for a time
A distraction
Then someone or something new comes along
Then some tragedy or hardship comes around
Then some self-inflicted wound is found
Discarded again, outside this time
No protection from the elements
Acts and words never meant
But the Throw-a-ways are
Resilient
Hearts broken in small pieces
But each piece has its own light

Strong enough to regenerate the whole

The Throw-a-ways
Rarely asked if anything is needed
Rarely asked if something is broken
Rarely asked if something can be done
Rarely listened to
Rarely asked to do less, only more
Rarely acknowledged
Rarely truly seen
Rarely fought for
Except when needed, wanted

Significance is conditional
Though the Throw-a-ways act and react without
Malice, indifference, distrust or disrespect
The others have a choice to be made
To treat with love and consideration or take the Throw-a-ways for granted
The dynamics always change, treated less and less important
Until
If and when
Discarded once again
The Throw-a-ways

Kimberly
8-2012

Agony

Agony, why do you continue to punish me
Taking hold of my body
I will never be broken, no matter the toll
You will never possess my soul

Danger Lies in the Past

Danger can be found and
Lies in the past and minds
In remembrance of
The past sins and mistakes
Past should be left alone

1984

Lost Soul

She was just one of those wandering lost souls
Where she emerged, no one knows
She can be seen under the lamppost
Standing or wandering all along the East Coast
Ever so famous, unfortunately in bad light
What her claim to fame is can be seen by sight
Scarlet hails red as young blood, eyes downcast around town
Beautiful skin no longer so, with the makeup of a clown
Lonelier than it could be imagined
The child abandoned by everyone was saddened

The nonchalant birth-giver to the best friend
To the law that gave up search
To the complacent citizens who sat back
And watched and whispered
Who all decided it was her destiny
The grave she dug for herself

1990

The Stone-yard

Petals from the roses glide through the air
Dust lightly layered the stone
Inscriptions of all kinds
Bent knees
Folded hands
Hands gracing marble
Tears
Forming patterns
Of sullenness
On grass surfaces
Showering tiny visitors
Shadowy forms
Creating human bonds
Unbeknownst
Unseen ones guarding
Loyal
Grief-stricken
Yet envious
Hell of living too much to bear
Jealous
Praying for sleep
Fog entrapping
But
Eventually comforted by the sun

Hunting Season

The only one of its kind
All year round
Wide bright eyes to find
Cracking twigs surround
In all ways and phases
The worst hunt of all
Hate saturates phrases
Dogs answer the call
Legs don't move as quick
Fear devours and slows
The darkest, strongest they'll pick
Piercing him with arrows from bows
Literal and not
Laughter of the animals
His hope is spiritual
They are like cannibals
Prayed not to be the target, treason
Because of his blackness, his difference,
His being is the reason
That he and his own, are the big game, of this year-round hunting season.

Darkness Disguises the Sun

Darkness disguises the sun
Always the one to shun
Waiting on a moment to seize
I crawl on hands and knees
Searching
Out-stretched hands
I hear voices
Looking for direction
Looking for the strong, loving hands
To grab me
To lift me
To take me home
Halted by something
Haunted
Engulfed by something
No, someone
The air changed
The estranged and deranged

I reached up with one hand
The other hand feels pressure
A shoe, a high heel pierces my hand on the floor
Held in despair, unable to reach for the door
No longer shed rivers of tears, only a few drops
You are so cold, no emotion, the heart stops
You tell me you knew
Huuumph, the sullen songs of Badu
I would never amount to
Would never be you
Hatred soaked through
The envy to undo

Never heard I love you

Never heard I will help you
Never heard you are beautiful
Never heard you are plentiful
Never heard I am here now and always
Well, don't matter now, no ways

I heard
Back down
Bow down
Face down
From Daddy — a Slap down
Stay down
I want to escape to Cape Town
Naw, this is
Where you belong
Who do you think you are?
Morally reprehensible
What happen to unconditional?
I heard
Not hardly cute
Now who's the brute?
Not nearly smart
What you know about art
Look at you
Tall and skinny, all legs
Dance?
Dance for what?
Dance for whom?
And college, Please
Such a tease

The heel removes itself
The one that does not love and just despises
All 24/7 chastises
Sashays in the opposite direction

The transgression
In the fetal position
Holding what's left
So much taken by theft
Keeping the pieces
Self decreases

In the corner, it is bright
A pinhole of light
Need to take flight
Crawl towards it
Finger enters, and tears
Blood smears
Opens wider
No need to hide her

A haven opening
Welcoming hands motioning
Another world in Europe
Who do you see?
A police officer, a guard
They love me?
So is this what love feels like?
One of the few females and with body for days
Thank God for the Air Force
A change, of course

What? I can't hear you.
Don't think it's true
I can't do what?
Money, Attraction, admiration…
Even from them, all right
I'll take it
No castration
Never a pay cut

Love the crew cut
So far so good
So damn good
Burning the wood
I withstood
Never want to go home
Never want to be alone

Home to storms and lightning
Where there is no enlightening
Natural disasters
Not a tornado or hurricane
No appreciation for the sugar cane
Natural disasters from
Natural blood ties
At home
To my heart
All apart
To my essence
No convalescence
For my being
To my soul
Never told
Thank God for the Air Force
Heard my voice

Germany was the beginning, the performance and an audition

Stage 3, curtain lifts
Time drifts
A daughter, a mini-me
Daughter in tow
No money, much woe
Back home to natural disasters

No welcome home ceremony
Sick of just eatin macaroni
How to make it now. Gotta hustle
Work that smooth muscle
Gotta work my hand, work that....
Minds and bodies twisted
Music banging
Women glaring
What part of the game is this?
How can I resist?
I can dance
I don't care about what's showing
I dance
I am a dancer
That's what I do
Hhummpphh
Just add high heels and lingerie
I'm good
No fear, no doubts
You said you knew, you knew I would
I know I got it
I know they want it
Eyes held at attention
Transition

Watch the hands
Hands move
One on the wallet the other
Around a bottle of champagne
And around my waist
Get him intoxicated with champagne
Get him intoxicated from me
Ain't nothing free
No need to agree
Just get the mon-ey

Every day, all day.
Every day, It's all sha-day

Behind the R & B, rap, rock, hip hop, whatever
The church music storms and rumbles
The sound of God, it humbles
It still captures me
Raptures me
But Pray
Pray for….. did He hear me?
We hungry
Gotta eat
Need shoes on feet
Gotta pay bills
Do what I have to
If it kills
Pray
Where **HE** at

When the Lights were off
Locked doors
Smoke galore
Money flows, so easily dispose
Music bump
Booties hump
Others sway
Other way
Deception of
A good life
What do you see?
A ho, a foe
The weak, discreet
The child, defiled
A toy soldier
Get bolder

Animalistic prey
Hard to say
Waiting for money- holding, sexual predators
Just a CEO, an editor or creditors

Prowling across the stage
Crawling across green paper
Still looking for
The strong, loving hands
To grab me
To lift me
To take me home
High heel impression still on hand
All I get is him

Lust filled
Reaching for me
I back away

I back away into the sun
My children reside there
The church
The sinners made to feel so....
I love God too!!
Not accepting, not good enough
Just like she said

And in the beginning...God created one that was less
One that was unworthy
She was right...
No, no
Back into the sun
There is another light
Star bright
She is beauty, She is pure

Not judging
Full of strength and love for me
She moves me, She encourages me
And it was good
But the Godly said
It was bad
The RIGHTIOUS are not accepting of
ALL of God's children
Not us
Heathen, hot-ass mess you say
Are you really lookin' this way?
I love as God said to love, God is love
I love what and whom I love
At least **I** Love
But
No one loves me

But the children and she
Sorry to disappoint you, it's not a he
Hypocrites
You refuse to show me God's mime
White face
White gloves
White soul
You refused to share

Said I needed Jesus, ok, I am here
show me
Take me there
Rejection

Head down, Eyes downcast
Tall frame bent down
To half size
Not crawling but low and cautious

No longer as dark
Hands reaching out
The high heel is not there this time
Tiny hands
Grab me
Tiny hands lift me
Not one, but two pair
Small arms hold me
They pull me up, straight and tall
The small angels from God
They taught me God's mime
They loved
Adored
Respected

Not the congregation
Not Mommy and Daddy
Just my babies and

And she

I hear music; all kinds
God's sounds and the sinners
Darkness disguises the sun
The white face and hands disguise me
The mask and motions
 R**eveal** who I am

A path lit by
Moonlight and torches
Directing to a new world
Beaches
Palm trees
My God
Church, uuughh I don't know

Church is **within** me
No longer a structure of suffocation and torture

Housing hypocrites inflicting pain
Those that shamed me
God loves me still
HE loved and protected me when I did not believe in him
When I seduced and stole
To keep full, their bowl
Where was the church roll?
When I doubted and cursed
He protected when I was followed in the dark and stalked
It was his guiding spirit and joyous feet that walked
He protected what was left of my heart when it was ripped open as a child
Made no never mind to him, I was riled, defiled, styled and buck wild
HE remained
When I left HIM
He carried me to 100 miniature angels
To teach them
These angels held me together
When I could not get THE one who should
To hold me forever

In a new world
A universe of God, children, love, and mime
There is light
There is peace
There is me
Am I really here?
The darkness still disguises the sun
But not so completely
I am no longer searching for that which hides from me
No longer searching for the pair of hands that bore me

Want it yes; painful yes, but I have some peace about it now
The darkness still disguises
But now I have matches, lighters, and torches
I have faith
I have strength
I have the will
To teach
To preach
To create
A fire
To see
To love
To praise
To move
To care
To ignite

That which died out in me
To share with thee
It is time to exclaim and reclaim
And rise once more in spiritual flames

8/21/10

Every Day I Fight to Walk in the Eyes of the Lord

Every day I fight to walk in the eyes of the Lord
For I have been taunted, hurt
The faith is trying to survive
Resentment and ill-will kept low, trying
Difficult
How can you not feel anger, hate even
After such a thing
It will never leave me
Yet walks away happily
God, please restore my body. Heal
God, I need not a father at this late date
But keep me from hating the poor excuse
Keep me from hating the wrong
Loves of my life since past
I should have stood alone
But it was your will to love
 Rescue souls

The right ones or not
If a man is not a father to his child
How could it be she will find a man?
To have a respectable, loving mate
Her father was not there, flesh and blood, kin.
How will any man truly be
Where is the faith
God, it is said it is your will to marry
Make the Earth plenty to prosper
To love, have faith, hope, to heal, to live

If such is your will, such it will be

1990

I Am

I am still and show no feelings
I see through the glass
They watch with interest
I sit trapped in metal
No one cares, neither do I
The priest stands by
He'd performed his service, as though it were memorized
I look in the window and see the switch
I see the hand moving in slow motion
Ever so slowly it moves, to its destiny and mine

1987

II.

Him, Her and Them

Crushing

Sound of the voice
So strong
Vibration of the words
Through the body
Heat generated
Through sound
And thoughts
The beauty and intensity of his song
Transcends

Action and reaction
Ignites
Inner flames
Long burned out
All senses awakened
Crushing feeling surrounds
The entire body
But not wanting to escape
Mind overwhelmed
Body in overdrive
Every inch pulsating
No warning of the
Speed, the force, and the magnitude
No escape
Crushing

6/28/12

Collapse

The sun was glorious, golden
Smiling over the Atlantic Ocean and Monrovia
Warm sand on the beach comforting beneath her feet
She stood alone but not
She felt his presence
She imagined how it could have been
Should have been
The look, the question the diamonds reflecting

Every one of the 1460 days played the same dream
Warmth, love, respect, peace, passion, loyalty, trust, laughter
Her soul mate always just out of reach
Believing if she proved how much she loved him and how good she was for him and with him
The walls would come down and the bridge from her heart to his, would be accessible
The Atlantic Ocean would become parted to his homeland allowing her to walk there
Walk to his heart and with the key to open it
She would jump in
Nestled in his warmth forever
As she stood the light became dim the sun not so warm
The wind became strong and unbearable trying to lift and carry her away
1460 days became 1461, 1462, 1463, 1464.........
The bridge became weaker and began to tremble
The walls of water began to collapse and so did her heart and soul

Love is not Supposed to Kill You

Love doesn't hurt
Only if you lose it
Love is not supposed to stab your heart
Or stab you in the back
Love does not scream profanity
But screams joy
Announcing its presence
Love does not ridicule
Does not deceive
Love doesn't whisper and laugh behind your back
Love is not about causing illnesses
It's sharing, caring, and opening up
It's putting the other person first
Love is to hate hurting one's love
Love does not stomp on your heart
Love does not entail games of the mind
Just growth of the two minds together
Melting souls
Love is not chest pains after the lie you were told
Love is not the non-ringing phone
After the broken promises
Love is not supposed to murder
Your heart, love, soul, dreams
It is not

1994

Transition

In the beginning love overwhelmed
Passion was in abundance
All words and sounds were in love and kindness
Embraced me
Your Actions evoked a wanting
Best interest at heart
Sharing without thinking
Time was precious and given in trust and safe keeping
Your smiles illuminated the night
Time passes

Transitions

Less likely to say a kind word
Passion still overflows but with caution
Words on occasion are laced with thorns
Desirable actions replaced by distance
And nonchalant motions
Time escapes in darkness and emptiness
No one is there

Infrequent and short
No matter, I will still remember the good and deal with the bad. My love will never die although my heart has died during this transition where
The beautiful voice that was melodic is now sullen and dry
The lips that loved to be kissed now hiss without thought

When Will It Be?

When will it be?
The love that embraces and devours
That protects and caresses
That soothes and moves
Bodies entwined in permanent bond
Suffocating yet pleasurable
Nothing exists around just he and I
When will it be?
The love that is deserving
The trust, the truth, the respect, the real
The love that does not involve pain
The love that only lifts
The spirit empowers the two
When will it be?
Both deserving
Lifelong happiness
Not a temporary remedy
There is undeniable chemistry
Mastermind of mixtures that will erupt
When will it be?
The unconditional love
That makes them want to be
the man or woman each should be
When will it be?
The irresistible love
Passion inflames
To an excruciating level
When will it be?

Quiet

Why are you so quiet?
He had an answer
Why not?
He is not seen
He is not heard
No matter how clear
No matter how loud
Why are you so quiet?
She did hear him say
I love you
She smiled with a certain
Look in her eyes
Already taking it for granted
Why are you so quiet?
Thoughts, words and behavior
He shows his loyalty
How much he cares
How much he loves
How much he understands
How much he respects
His strength
The others disregard
No acknowledgement
Of their wrongs
No point anymore, telling how he felt
When he is angry or hurt
And does the mature thing and
Expresses
No acknowledgement, no apology
No accountability on behalf of others
As if nothing was spoken
Nothing, by a nobody
He must be quiet.

10/12

The First Time Won't Be the Last

The first time he asks you why it took you so long to get home from work won't be the last
The first time he goes through your phone and demands you delete all male contacts won't be the last
The first time he forces you to have sex won't be the last
The first time he calls you fat and ugly won't be the last
The first time he makes you change your clothes, won't be the last

The first time he limits time you spend with family and friends won't be the last
The first time he calls you stupid won't be the last
The first time he calls you a bitch won't be the last
The first time he embarrasses you in front of others won't be the last
The first time he shoves you into the table won't be the last
The first time he slaps you in the face won't be the last
The first time he punches you in your side, won't be the last
The first time he kicks you won't be the last
The first time he chokes you won't be the last

The first time he threatens to do something to your children won't be the last
The first time he yells at your children won't be the last
The first time he hits your children won't be the last
The first time he threatens to kill you won't be the last
The first time he attempts to kill you won't be his last
It will be the last time when you check him and walk away the very first time

The Look, the Sound

There was a side-glance
Down the aisle
The eye scan has been perfected
Lowest price, best quantity
Thirty in hand
Decisions
Half a tank of gasoline
The Look
Mother smiles wide at child
Sticky fingers grabbing treats
The smile does not reach the eyes

The look
Strain
Forced peace
For the child's sake
Worry lines from the eyes to the heavens
One hand on the cart one hand on the little shoulder
She is unaware how many times
She sighed since walking into the store
Mind calculating
Planning ahead

She hears a voice
Strong
Deliberate
Weighted
The sound
She sees the man
Moving quickly down the aisle
The sound
Exhausted
Yet focused

A little boy in the cart
The little girl holding onto the bottom
Of his work shirt
Aged with motor oil
Rust stains
Rips and tears
Work pants faded but creased

But the little ones are
Immaculate
Clean
Matching outfits
 Ponytails a little lop-sided

But the braids are neat.
Even the little boy, under two
Appeared to have a haircut
The mother smiles
They seem happy
He has the look
Alone
But determined
There are periodic flickers
Of disbelief in the eyes
How did we get here?

She could tell he worked hard
His work boots were surprisingly clean
She caught his eye and smiled with
Understanding
Encouragement
He responded with a warm
Half smile
But the eyes revealed more

Without thinking as she pushed
Passed his cart, she
Reached out to the child in the seat
He grabbed her thumb
She winked at the little girl
Her son moved in closer
He looked at the lil' one
Looked at the man
Looked at his mom
She gave a final look at the
Dad
And moved on

She did not look back
He watched her walk away
Her little boy looked back at him
Almost with one eyebrow raised
The Dad smiled from ear to ear,
He looked into his children's eyes
He moved on
He would remember
She felt his gaze
She would remember

10/2012

The Spirit

I wonder did Jonah feel like this
Totally embodied by the whale
Dark, yet no fear because of the Spirit
Safe, warm, in such appearance
Of threat
That is what it feels like
Love swallows you whole
No way out. But you are safe
Like the whale, so large and strange
You fear it
Wonder how he felt
Do you feel it, I love you. You love me
Engulfed, defenseless
No desire to defend
Take us

2-11-94

Invade Her Thoughts

How can it be that she has allowed
One to invade her thoughts
A dangerous thing for her
A little too close to the heart
Will he descend?
Will he slowly take the stairs, the elevator?
Or will he leap from the edge of her brain
Into the most precious and vulnerable
Part of her heart and soul
She is a woman of unconditional love
Unlimited empathy, passion, and compassion
To share with the one unworthy
Could prove deadly
She lost so much already
Not much left for her
Who will make emotional deposits?
To rebuild her account once again
For she is in the negative

Taken for granted and disrespected
Loneliness has become norm
Not so difficult to tolerate
A way of life
Better than perhaps the alternative
A history she prefers to forget
But must be embraced,
So as to avoid a repeat

So unusual, this one

He makes her smile
He makes her laugh
He makes her consider
He does not judge or condescend
But how would he feel
What would he think?
After he knows all
Sees all
That which is behind
A photo he likes from long ago

He is unusual
Holds one's interest
He inspires
Intellectual and emotional
Lovemaking is just as powerful

She knows all are different
Cannot judge or assume
She is epitome of love, loyalty and strength
The strength forms barriers
Cement walls too high and too wide
Fear of unknown grip like a chokehold
She can decide whether to break free

To be continued….

4/2012

Desire to Forget but Not Forgive

Eyes Closed
I could not stand to look in those cold eyes
Who could this be?
Certainly not the man of my dreams
Whom I loved unconditionally

Eyes closed
There was a hard pull
Hit the floor
How many times had we made love on this floor
Now there's only blood on this floor
Breath held for another blow, tear
Pleading. Anger Intertwined with fear

Eyes Closed
Reached for the phone, hair pulled, head yanked back
What was that chilling sound, my neck?
Items thrown about, where's my check?
Not the face, can't hide that, need to react
That damn brute
Despised brown boot
Destined for its target
Print on cheek
A shriek

Eyes closed
Never afraid before
That is what is most hated, not the pain the terror
Used to be such a fighter
In the matter of minutes, diminished to nothing, error
Years ago, yet so vivid

Eyes closed
Lied about your age
Lied about umpteen women scorned
Thought I was having your firstborn
So many little ones already existed
So many big lies already twisted

Eyes closed
Did not matter how good I was
How intelligent I was
How faithful I was
How cute I was

How well dressed I was
How nice my hair was
How catering I was
How understanding
How withstanding
How sincere
How revered
How caring
How sharing
How powerful
How independent
How resplendent
How sweet
How…

Eyes closed
Wore that nice pink silk suit that day
Waited for you to take me to the job
Waited, never came
Took two buses to and from
Walked with shame
Accusations when the door slammed

Where were you?
He was laid up somewhere I am sure
Yet fingers pointed at me
Not the least bit demure
Yet fists were laid on me
Dirty words were hurled at me
Feet danced and stomped on me

Eyes closed
Back on the floor
Arms held down by digging knees
I was suddenly cold
I began to freeze
Tried to get to the door
Lamp held over my face
God No, evil voice, nasty names
God No, evil voice, horrific claims
What is this place, this cannot be my fate
Need to get out of this hell
Where Satan dwells
Brain functioned again, made a move
Escaped
As if it were yesterday, as if it were today
If only I had something with which to slay

Eyes opened
God gave me a gift, salvation
A little angel inside, saved me
From this condemnation
It was so easy to run
No heavy weight, no indecision
Peace for mine was the envision
What could be more important than protecting the angel?
Even though he had not arrived on this earth as of yet
I may have remained a moment too long in this threat

What if he had not passed through me?
As if it were yesterday
Unwanted and undesired, away through sieving
Shadows loom dark, choking and unforgiving
Will God forgive me, if I don't forgive?
Eyes closed

Written in 2008, in regards to 1994

Healing Touch

A touch by you
Moves me
A word, a loving phrase
Soothes me
My hand in yours
Generates electrifying heat
The sound of your voice
Melts the ice in my heart
Your laughter
Chisels away at the wrath I have
When you hold me
I only remember what is good
I look in your eyes
I see all and accept
You kiss me
My body trembles
You love me
I am empowered
We are empowered
Staring into eyes
Hands on my face
Healing touch

2008

Dance

We dance in harmonious seclusion
In our own world
Gazes never waiver
Unbreakable connection
With each step and motion
Darkness illuminated
By the light from your eyes and smile
Intensity unbearable
We are whatever we need to be
To each other, at any given time
What is it you need
Sister, best friend, lover, confidant
Shock waves
Unprepared but well received
Constant shivers still do not
Affect the dance
Enhances
Unmistakable
The dance was meant to be
Right here, right now
With these two
Walls that were so clear and impossible
Both equally strong, pushing, pulling, holding
To overcome, have new openings, lowering
Dancing around, above, below, and through
For which to allow some peace
Love, happiness, and faith

2010

Helicopter

Every night she lay in wait
Beside the window
She will always tempt fate
Face on silk pillow

Eyes half closed
The sound
So imposed
Heart bound

The helicopter
It hovers
It opts for her
Under covers

He comes up
Singing
She comes down
Feigning

She knew he would be there
Eventually
To affirm the affair
Sensually

4/2012

Fruits of Passion

The irresistible lips of the man I love, can't resist
The ones I ache for, the chill of ecstasy persist
His strong hands over mine, permeates me with security
Initiating the course of love, the true desire, purity
His intriguing eyes, the ones that melt me, putty in hand
Abduction, taking me into a whirlwind of tenderness
Only he can

The exquisite arms, embodying my soul, into a vision of rapture
His ability to engulf me in eroticism, illustrating his stature
His masculine legs, powerful, entangled around mine not wanting to let go
Moistened from a feverish aura of warmth, unctuous, oh, how I love it so
His firm back, withstanding the pressure, assiduous, so vigorous
Both searching and exploring, experimenting the new, so curious

The imaginable and unimaginable need to be mentioned
The fantasies and dreams, surrendering to reverie, leaves me in contention

Passion cannot be mistaken for anything less
The fruits of passion, only you possess

Love is Not Just a Word

I do

It is you that I love
It is you that I seek
God sent you from above
Intense passion you've peaked

I do believe this union is forever
I do promise to be honest
I do promise to bare my soul whenever
A blessed day in August
A family has been created
Far too long we have waited

Moves Me

So rare to look into one's eyes and be taken to another place
Eyes so deep and telling, yet not
Secrets
Mysteries
Waiting for me to discover
Lips that part with a deep soulful sound
Which vibrates over my body, over my soul
Dance that inspires me, to live, to sing, and dance

To breathe

Arms of strength, assurance, and trust
Lifting to salacious places
Smooth dark skin to be kissed with passion
The body that is man, virile, yet moves gracefully to the
Beats and rhythms
He controls it all, the tempo and the beats begin
to follow him
As he leads through turns, jumps, artistic but subtle
seductive moves

I become lost in his eyes and his movements
Body trembles with every look, every step,
Colorful motions of every part of his body
Head spinning, craving what is Liberian
Warrior
Confronting, prepared for every battle
Protecting what is his
Loving what is his
Adoring what is his
Inspiring, igniting

The flames within
To dance, to move free

Forbidden

What is forbidden
She saw the beautiful African man
The eyes snatched her first
His face his body she scanned
Instant hunger and thirst

Forbidden by the number of years
Too many hard journeys
Much said, so many sneers
Old lady on gurney

Her desire and passion always been strong
She is hard to satisfy physically
Not matchable by one half her age
She is hard to satisfy intellectually

Is the forbidden one the one?
Half her age, with interests of those his age
Will he be likely to run?
Away from someone at this stage
She sees through him
There is depth and he is a dime
Does he see through her
The depth, but also the wearing of time

The heaviness that once was tight and firm
Would love be made in the dark, with thoughts of
Another, more youthful time, confirm
Or love and appreciate the experience of

That which is forbidden

Out of Reach

Unspoken words were so clear
She watched his every move
Every expression
She imagined the hands of precision
The skills they must have

The vibration of stick to drum
Riveted through her body
She wondered how he could be so focused on her
And not miss a beat

She longed for long talks
During the long walks
She had not laughed so much
Been so long
What was this connection?
This almost instant understanding
From 1192 miles away
He was right here but he wasn't
Over 18 hours away
So out of reach

So unfair how life has its
Twists and turns and jokes it seems
To be introduced to what you may have
Been looking and longing for
Only to have it out of touch
Out of reach.
She envisioned looking up
At her giant and he looking down
Admiration and care

No pretense

So appealing
A father
She can feel the love of his children
It radiates through his words
More importantly high actions
There is an intense vibe of sincerity
So many are part-time
Or no-time
No respect or love for the gifts given to them
God entrusts us with babies
He is fulfilling what he has been asked to do

18 hours 47 min
1190.16 miles

Tall
Drummer
Laughter
Warm
Father
Proud
Conscious
Intense eyes
Dreams
Risk taker
School, music, technical, artistic
Prince and princess
Quiet
Saying very little
Yet revealing much

The Other Freedom

Legs intertwined
Head on chest
Silk ties bind
Wrists protest

Lips explore
Spoken
Every door
Open

Aroma
Intoxicating
Corona
Frustrating

Cannot devour
Enough
Another hour
Rough

Inhibitions
Buried
Munitions
Carried
Positions
Varied
Conditions
Wearied

But smiles
Through trials

For miles
To British Isles

Rendezvous
For two
Sexual debut
Anew

6/2012

Song

Your words ride on the tail of emotions
The sweet sounds set to music
Inspirations pull you toward
Expression
Pen seems to have a mind of its own
Flowing those sweet love songs
Sowing the seeds
Of a musical genius

We Will Always Be

Thousands of miles away
Beyond the oceans
Beyond continents
We will still be one
The bond will never collapse
Never ending alliance
A breach will never come to pass
You can be in someone else's arms
In the bed of many
One can have your name
I will always be with you, you will feel me
We are inescapable

2008

What Feels Good

What feels good
Being loved though you may not fully love yourself
What feels good
Is knowing that he knows
All of your secrets, imperfections and fears
But he loves you still
He takes all the lumps, bumps and scars in your life
On your body, in your heart, in your soul
And he embraces the essence of you
As if it is the most precious, as if it is priceless
He sees you and beyond
He understands, he respects, he accepts
What feels good
Knowing his secrets and imperfections
And loving him still
Being allowed into his world and loving all
That there is
Accepting his good, bad, and ugly
Being able to be you and enhancing his life
And he enhancing yours

Knowing after a long hard day at work
When he comes home, it is you he finds solace in
When he comes home, it is him you find solace in
Both leaving love notes and words of encouragement
Poems, songs and scriptures
Praying together, believing together
Watching TV together, listening to music together
Cooking together, eating together
Dancing together, laughing
Crying together, fussing together

Playing together, Bathing together
Communicating about any and everything
There is no hesitation, you are free to be
Who you are, around one another
No guilt

What feels good
Being in the same room
Not touching, not speaking, not even looking at each other
But having the most intimate moment
What feels good
Knowing what words to say to him
Knowing when to just listen and not offer advice
Knowing he has had his challenges today
And he just needs to be held
Not judged, not demanded to do anything
But just be for tonight
He knows when to do the same for you

What feels good
Being separate
Playing the other roles demanded
Of you but still loving and understanding
Understanding and appreciating space
Other commitments and obligations
No jealousy, no insecurities
Only admiration for all that one has to do
Knowing that you both, willingly and excitedly come home

What feels good
Is growing together
Learning together
Teaching each other
Sharing, to be matched intellectually
He does not think less of you and your abilities

He shares his knowledge and skills
He is proud when you pick up something
That he has taught you
An extension of him, an extension of each other
You are proud to share something
With him and he has found use and appreciation

What feels good
He is a man, you are a woman
You do not have to think for him
You do not have to tell him what you need
You do not have to tell him what you want
But if you do, there is no issue
He is just that tuned into you. As you are to him
He has listened; he has looked and truly seen
He has evaluated
Knowing that he will find solutions
And you will find solutions together
What feels good

What feels good
Knowing that he is a father
He has put his children first
They are so much a part of him
He understands putting others above him
He understands being there, being unselfish
He loves what you have done on the home front
With yours and respects your children
And knowing the cherished gift of these earth angels
Family
He loves you enough to make you
A part of this and allows you to contribute

What feels good
Walking in the park

Meditating together
Exercising together
Going to the doctor together
And he simply holding your hand
Understanding and saying it is ok, that he is here
God will keep you and so will he

What feels good
Crying for an hour about something
Later looking at the phone
There is a missed call
It is him
Tears dry up
You call
Something in the sound of his voice, in his words
You hear every word, every inflection, and every pause
Every level of volume, every not-so-hidden emotion
It causes you to forget what you were crying about in the first place
If only for a moment

What feels good is thinking of him
Whenever, wherever
And not being able to breathe
How can that be?
To not know him but yet you do
To not hold him, to not touch him
But yet you are
To not be in his presence, to not look into his eyes
But you feel as though every part of your body
Has been massaged and caressed by him
You have gone limp and you are unable to breath
What the hell is that? And Why?
Some things are not meant to be questioned
No matter, no matter at all

You just don't want it to end

4/27/2012

What You Deserve, What I Deserve

Your heart has been broken like mine
You have been disrespected and taken for granted
Now is the time
For what you deserve

A woman to recognize
Your strengths and weaknesses
And love you still
To hold you and work with you
Instead of against you
To appreciate your sacrifices and
For her to make a few of her own
For the US, For WE, For the OUR

No longer do you have to accept
Or settle for less
To keep up appearances
Or for the sake of others
You can give freely
Without advantage and
Receive without a tally
Show affection, love and solidarity openly
Damn the world

You deserve that peace
When all else is being destroyed
Falling apart and
Breaking into little pieces
But you stand together
The TWO should be able
To find comfort in the other

Your home is your place of solace
Your solace is your love
Let nothing stand in your way
Of attainment

6/28/2012

III.

When You Feel Like Giving Up, Don't

Resurrection — The Voice

No I'm not crazy
I have not broken under the pressure
I am no longer hiding
I am no longer quiet

Liberated
I know what I want and need
I am no longer afraid
Making it known
You do not have to like or love it
It does not hurt me
It does not make me angry

This is not acceptable
You are not acceptable
I will not try to change you
I will not try to make you fit
I will not re-adjust
Believing it will make you accept me
Love me, do right by me
Or be dismissed
I wish you the best
I still care
But you must move on
Be gone

I never lost my voice
But the voice was silent
I put a muzzle on myself
I had a hand, along with so many other people
And cold circumstances wrapped around my throat
Darkness of doubt and pain placed me in a bear hold

Held me still
All was stagnant
I recovered and revived self-love, my strength, my worth

Resurrection

Natural, and It's Ok

Clarity
You no longer have to feel bad
You no longer have to apologize
You love
They do not love you back the same way
And it's Ok.
Clarity
You can love, but not too much
At least not with the wrong person for you
Loving in abundance is fine
With the person that loves you in abundance
They do exist
You must be patient
It is ok
If you are liking and loving more than the other person
Show even more love for yourself by letting them go
You are expressing love by allowing them to find someone they can be in love with

Do not become discouraged or angry
Be patient with you
It takes time
Have self-compassion
Self-forgiveness
You do not have to subject yourself to pain and discomfort
Stop dwelling
Behavior will reflect how one feels about you
You do not want or need to MAKE someone feel the same as you
Create the best possible relationship with YOURSELF
Than receive someone else in to share it

Natural progression is beautiful
Natural flow without pushing and pulling
It's enjoyable, fun, exciting, peaceful, whole
Natural

Never Lose Yourself

Never let them drift away in a whirl of wind
The dreams and goals, aspirations, you
Through my eyes, talent left to rot is a sin
Determine, we must, our lives, a clue

There are many talent-filled, but shiftless
Knowledge abounds, the potential, but trapped, forsaken
Obstacles, low self-esteem, the plagues, one less
Not I, I declare, not a piece but the pie I have taken
Your foundation, your chance, that foot in the door, you must create
When an opportunity knocks, rend the door from its hinges
Never lose the faith that carries you, never wait
Perhaps I am extreme, one of the few, one of the fringes

Let us hasten together through the narrow opening, I transmit
Let us, not just I, remember the rest, fulfill the ultimate
I am only sure of one truth, my destiny
And as I rise, you shall rise with me.

Blessings

Do you hear the light thumping? It's not your heart
Rhythms so smooth, they are a part
of you.
Joyous blessings from God, it can only be seen this way
What mixed emotions, shock, when you found out that
day

Fortunate or not, so it must be seen. The lies inside
Right or wrong they are yours this cannot hide
Two bundles of miracles, two gifts from God wrapped
in love
How can any negative, any shadows plague these from
above

As hard as it may be, remember the unconditional love
is there
Through the sleepless nights, ugly stares, whispers you
may bear
Believe in you. Believe in the little ones, this trio comes
first
Keep your head held high and seek joy in the love they
thirst

1-14-93

Benevolence

A rainbow of colors filtered through the glass
A sight of joy as if nature knew
A beautiful day of hope, blessings did not pass
The tiny gift from Him, awaiting the dew

How overjoyed you must be, taking part in this miracle
To have created and loved this one, such innocence
Never to have been touched by sin, tears a trickle
Needing only what God wanted for us, love, benevolence

Hearing the mini heartbeats, feeling the first punt
Knowing that the breath is just a whisper in its domain
The thought that the daily nourish will not be a hunt
For your gifts to thee are as great, no one could defame

We welcome the offspring with open arms of unconditional love
We welcome the birth in jubilee like the birth of Christ in history
We welcome the ritual of miniature feet from above
We welcome the dancing eyes, babble and gurgles of sweet melody

IV

The Son—His Words

I'm Me

Devoted young man attempting to
Elevate his character to have a
Voice in this world. Proving that his
Opinions matter.
Not to be rude by all means, but it's
True. I just believe
Everyone should know me.

The Forgotten

I am grass blades upon beautiful flowers
I am an antelope in the savannah dark
I am far past my youthful days
I am a dull black that isn't considered a color to scientists
I am a loner, drifter, constantly on the move
I am water being polluted, allowing anything and everything within me
I am hopeless with no goals for myself that set me apart

Goodbye, Lebron

Taking my talents to south beach he said
To only wither when times become rough
Get them to the playoffs and play dead
You soon realized the playoffs are tough

Five years have passed and she still wants to wed
What can I say to string my love along?
Hey a ring before the king I said
Should buy me some years for Lebron's wrong

Scared of two shots at the line that are free
The greats never crumble under pressure
You don't deserve greatness if you ask me
So the players we have I'll treasure

Cleveland doesn't want you anymore you see
So go along and leave both you and Z

Bright Lights

Step back and consider the night's bright lights
A lonely feeling it may seem
Until you look at the moon's tiny beam
Casting a bright stage upon the dark night
Perhaps a glimpse of a full moon you might
See a taste of people a tad bit mean
Did you see this moon? Tell me if you seen
The beautiful night of the night's bright lights

Critters prowl the darkness on the night stage
Going about their daily lives and tasks
Giving purpose to a wonderful sight
To mingle among themselves and engage
the festivities that the moon unmasks
So tell me, have you seen the night's bright lights?

Love Lost

My heart, be strong and do not falter so
Nor beat with such struggle, I'm so frail!
Your love is excruciating, I know
But I won't begin to whither and fail

Understand why Shakespeare couldn't compare
His once true love to a mere summer's day
To stumble upon such beauty is rare
You leave me speechless, no words can I say

A stranger you once were; a foreigner too
With one gentle, soft touch you became known
So nervous I didn't know what to do
But a new life you've given me and shown

You remain in my heart that beats with pain
Keeping my heart under tremendous strain

Love in Basketball

A basketball, my basketball
Symbolizes much more
Though through the common eyes of mere fans
It's a symbol beyond comprehension

Nicks on a basketball, my basketball
Possesses scars proving a hard fought season
The rounded sphere it holds
Shows of never giving in
A sphere is a shape our earth beholds
So I will become global after this final game

What more can you ask for from a basketball, my basketball
Other than to make a sweet call
To reward me for an excellent shot through the net

Go ahead basketball, my basketball
Send the opposition a kiss off the glass
To give them a little finesse

The basketball, my basketball
Forces the crowd to wait
My ball called to me....
56-58

Just Dance

Your spring green,
Juicy leaves provide
A pretty scene.
Dancing and prancing
Around branches
Like MJ in
His prime. Await
Your time to
Shine and land
On the
Soil dance floor.

Purple Hood

How tall and dangerous I stood
With a symbol on my purple hood
You'd just erase me if you could
You run fast and yes, you should
I'm too smart and slick and good
You see black eyes of the true hood
You see brown skin, I wish you would
See
The speed at which I read
The knowledge I wish to feed
Under the hood I dream of rhythms
Not raps but poems of like, great minds
The purple of royal kings of past
Essence of strength will always last
Books of philosophy, math, and science
Weapons of intelligence and wit, defiance
As I continue to earn that 3 to 4.0…oh so bold
In my jeans and my hoodie of purple and gold

Stolen and Betrayed

The world truly distresses me
The world is being used up in so many ways
So many worries why can't we be free

Many young lives stolen by crime
Land being abused and people hungry for days
The world truly distresses me

How many will be left in a future time
The environment and animals, the human betrays
So many worries, why can't we be free

Rivers to cross and mountains to climb
While the rope of hope only frays
The world truly distresses me

Where will you be no longer in your prime
Nothing left but skeletons walking in a daze
So many worries, why can't we be free

If only for every effort and promise I had a dime
In glory or demise will we go in a blaze
The world truly distresses me
So many worries, why can't we be free

About the Author:

Kimberly L. Edge considered herself a serious writer at a very young age. She loves to read and write extensively. She is employed at Kent State University. She is also an entrepreneur and a full-time student. She enjoys spending time with her son, watching sporting events, plays, anything dealing with music, dance, creating crafts, traveling, helping others and learning new things.

She does not mind sharing her own personal struggles and experiences, if it can make a difference one person at a time. She translates what she sees and empathizes with, to provide a window and a mirror to souls. The truths of society, good and bad, are often unmasked. Her passion is reaching others who need to feel encouraged, inspired and motivated. Hopefully, one less person will feel alone. She is excited about sharing her poetry and other writing projects with the world.

Feel free to connect with Storm at the following:
Twitter: @QuietStormxKLE
Email: theuntouchablebusinessofwords@gmail.com
http://Theuntouchablepoet.weebly.com

A small collection from the teenage son of the author is also included in the book. His verses are reflective of the author's spirit, consciousness, and what or who is important.

www.ingramcontent.com/pod-product-compliance
Lightning Source LLC
Chambersburg PA
CBHW071226160426
43196CB00012B/2422